We Rise Higher

Poems and Prayers
for Graduates

JOE DAVIS

2022

To: Andrew
From: Your Church Family
First Presbyterian Church

Cover and interior image: Abstract painted background by Anegada.
    Copyright © iStock. Adapted by Kristin Miller.
Cover and interior design: Kristin Miller
Editor: Dawn Rundman
Project manager: Julie O'Brien

"The Need for Rest and Stillness" first appeared in *Staying Awake: The
Gospel for Changemakers* by Tyler Sit. "You Gotta Cry Sometimes" first
appeared in the Connect Journal of the ELCA Youth Ministry Network.

ISBN: 978-1-5064-8483-9
Manufactured in USA

26 25 24 23 22   2   3   4   5   6   7   8   9   10

This book is dedicated to
the next generation of
graduates who are showing
the world just how high
we can rise together.

To the Reader

I wouldn't have survived high school if it wasn't for how God showed up through my community. There were times when I felt alone in the struggle, and I wondered if anyone else shared my fears and doubts.

Will I even graduate? Will I trip and fall in front of everyone when I go onstage to get my diploma?

What happens next? What does "adulting" even mean, and do I have what it takes to make it in life? Am I enough?

How can I ever live up to all the expectations people have of me? Can I even live up to the expectations I have of myself?

Every single day we're bombarded with messages from media machines, assaulted by microaggressions, or unexpectedly bumping against unhealed wounds.

This is why I need prayers, practices, and community to remind me, and help me remind others, of who I am, who we are, and who we can become together.

Whenever I forget, I'm reminded of how the beauty and power of God lives within me because of the beauty and power of God I see reflected in you and those around us.

God is always moving within us.

The ways God shows up through prayers, practices, and community have always been what most powerfully transforms me and calls me to action. During my transition into the world after high school, I realized how much I needed these reminders. It was then that I learned not only did others share my fears and doubts, but they also shared my hopes and dreams.

My highest hope and biggest dream for you is that you live into the fullness of who God called and created you to be. I pray that all of who you are is not just tolerated but celebrated. l pray that you know your value doesn't decrease based on someone else's opinion—and that you know this truth so deeply within yourself that it vibrates in every cell of your being until you rise above any obstacle or challenge.

You are enough.
You are good and worthy of love.

You are whole just as you are in this very moment.
Nothing anyone says or does,
even yourself,
can ever change that.

You are filled with an infinite abundance
of grace, resilience, and brilliance
because this is who the Creator created you to be.

And if you ever forget, may the poems and prayers in this book serve as reminders of the beauty and power of God within you and your community.

Even if we fall, we fall in love. We catch each other, we hold each other.
Ultimately, we rise as high as we lift each other.

I rise, you rise,
you rise, I rise,
together
we rise higher.

Contents

Poems of Praise and Affirmation

This Place

A poem to honor where you feel most like you

Here is where we give you the permission you haven't yet given yourself
to show up and be
your most authentic self.

You can cry here,
you can take your time here,
to be you is not a crime here.

We are all divine here,
we shine brighter when we all shine here,
we rise higher when we all rise here,
we practice being kind here,
we celebrate the fact that we are still alive here.

You can make mistakes here,
no guilt, blame, or shame here,
there's only grace here,
we know you by name here,
we've been waiting for you,
so glad you came here,
we hope that you stay here,
all that you are can be reclaimed and embraced here.

An Invitation:

Place your hand over your heart, breathe
deeply, and thank God for the gift of your
body. What's the most compassionate thing
you can do for yourself in this moment?
Go and do that.

Gather

A poem calling you to gather up what matters

Re-member to gather your selves,
All the parts of you that have been forgotten and forsaken:

Gather joy in your soul,
gather wisdom in your spirit,
gather peace in your mind,
gather love in your heart,
gather healing in your body.

Re-member to gather our selves,
All the parts of us that have been forgotten and forsaken:

Gather your people,
gather those who have been made invisible,
gather those who have been made unheard,
gather those who are weak and weary,
gather those who are bound and broken.

Gather together,
beyond want and need,
hands stretched open, palms set free,
to call and respond, to give and receive.

An Invitation:

Think of times in your life when you've
gathered some of the things mentioned
in the poem. Set aside a small space where
you can gather a few items that remind you
of who and what matter most. Visit this
space as often as needed.

In Comparison

A poem about being enough

A forever-spinning competition-carousel,
a never-ending, non-stopping Ferris wheel:
"Will I ever be as good as everyone else?"
Try to be everything, but never myself.

Like a pair of children in comparison,
fighting over our parent's love,
like we're in the ring wearing a pair of gloves,
I can't bear to look,
it tears me up how it tears us up.
Someone's always one tier above—

Will we learn to live together or perish alone?
What shared legacy are we carrying on?

A forever-spinning competition-carousel,
a never-ending, non-stopping Ferris wheel:
"Will I ever be as good as everyone else?"
Try to be everything, but never myself.

Who's inferior
when the same earth cares for us and buries us?
Who's superior
when we all share the same air in our lungs?

The proof is right there in our thumbs:
a fingerprint marking that there is but one—

One you, one me, nothing compares to us,
ordinarily extraordinary and we are enough.

An Invitation:

Write a list of some things you love about yourself. Place this list on your bedroom nightstand, next to your bathroom mirror, or somewhere else you will see it often.

Believe

A prayer for self-confidence

If you call a butterfly a caterpillar
will she cease to fly at all,
or only if she doubts herself
will she then begin to fall?

If a caterpillar begins to dream
she has wings and can fly,
do her dreams become a chrysalis
to help her touch the sky?

An Invitation:

What pose or movement makes you feel most confident in your body? Spend five to ten minutes embodying this pose or movement and pay attention to how it makes you feel.

On Faith

A poem about trust in times of uncertainty

Faith is not a hapless, hopeless well-wishing
nor flicking pennies in a wishing well fishing
for whatever our shaking hands can hold.

Faith is moving forward,
if even in the dark,
if even fallen,
sometimes stumbling, groping, crawling,
following the unmistakable, unshakeable calling of the ones
who have gone on before us
because we trust
that they know the way
and they know us.

An Invitation:

Faith can mean trusting things will work
out even when you don't know how.

Think of some times when you didn't think
things would work out, but they did. Write
down these memories as reminders to
yourself when you need to hear them.

Prayer: Life

A prayer-poem to remind us Who's listening

I believe
whether we know it or not
we are always talking with God—

Laughing, weeping, raging, ranting,
eating, sleeping, daydreaming, dancing,

Everything above, below,
or in between
whispers and screams, mutters and moans, grunts and groans,
more than wagging tongues, ebbing lungs, and tickled throats,

Our bodies' language sings
letters and notes,
books printed on skin and bone,
sent back home,
delivered through space and time,

And each moment there is One who listens intently,
bends gently,
and responds in kind.

An Invitation:

Spend one day intentionally looking
for how God might be speaking to you
through your body, the people around
you, scripture, and nature. Write down
what you notice.

Poems of
Joy and
Celebration

Gratitude

A song of thanks to God and others

This one thing I have for you,
it's not automatic or a magic pill, it's gradual.
I know the sadness grabs us all,
but we don't have to fall.
We ain't got it all together, but together we got it all:

Holler hallelu!
We call it gratitude!
In all I say and all I do—
the more I think of thanks
the more I think of you, I think of you.
The more I think of thanks the more I think of you!

My gratitude is radical,
sends my sadness on sabbatical,
when battling my shadows it's the greatest tool I know!

I was crying but I'm laughing now.
It can alter any mood or attitude, when I'm out of tune it's my autotune,
it taught me how to move my altitude like a ladder to a hot air balloon!

I don't always know what to do,
I don't always have a choice,
but you choose me,
and I receive to give joy and rejoice:

Holler hallelu!
We call it gratitude!
In all I say and all I do—
the more I think of thanks
the more I think of you, I think of you.
The more I think of thanks the more I think of you!

Always be grateful for all things
because almost all change is small change in small ways.

All praise to Yahweh for all of my days,
give proper props to God in all that I say.
Honor the fallen and all of them we follow today—
ancestors who paved the way, we call them by name.

It's okay to not be okay,
we all go through pain
but whether sun rays or some rain
one thing is the same:

Holler hallelu!
We call it gratitude!
In all I say and all I do—
the more I think of thanks
the more I think of you, I think of you.
The more I think of thanks the more I think of you!

An Invitation:

Write a letter thanking a friend, teacher, parent, or mentor who has impacted your life. Consider giving it to them.

Kinship

A poem to honor friends

Whenever I am lost and forget who I am,
I am greeted with our friendship,
tracing like a map,
fingertip on fingerprints
pointing me to the
re-collection of memories,
back to our first love, our purpose, where our purest intention is,
the reason for our existence.

I find the outline of our fingerprints
while sitting, talking, eating lunch.
I do this in re-membrance
for the times when I keep forgetting that,
as we all forget,
"I" am an extension of "us."

Just you and me, sipping coffee or tea,
when gathered something sacred stirs in the midst.
In this moment our presence is the truest gift,
since the beginning what has sustained and strengthened us
has always been in "us."

No need to be siblings to share this sacred lineage.
No need to look alike to bear a family resemblance.
We're not forsaking the assembly of ourselves,
we re-assemble ourselves with each other's help.

We are all descendants ascending into this kinship.
Whether shed or shared,
no blood is as thick.
When we reminisce, we revisit home,
more alive and less alone.

An Invitation:

Call or text a friend just to let them
know how much you appreciate them.
If you can, surprise them with a gift you
know they will love.

This Joy

A prayer for joy

This joy is a practice
this joy is habit
this is a birthright
and can't nobody snatch it

More than happiness, it's an everlasting bliss
because we survived everything that ever happened to us

We slayed demons and dragons
overcame obstacles and challenges
with bruised feet and callused hands
they wonder how we dance
they ask us how we can still smile like this

Children of the Most High, royal descendants
fresh heirs, we reign and shine
bringing sight to the color-blind,
can I get a witness?!

This is joy unspeakable, joy unending
our very existence represents this joy's persistence

Skin glistenin', fist lifted, singing for all those listening
the world can't take this joy because the world didn't give it.

An Invitation:

Make a Jar of Joy. On small strips of paper, write words or phrases that describe what brings you joy. Place these in a jar and feel free to give or take from the jar as needed. To spread the joy, invite others to give or take from the jar.

Poems
for Heavy
Emotions

You Gotta Cry Sometimes

A poem about tears

I sat in silence on the edge of my bed,
with traffic jam thoughts piling inside of my head,
nerves vibrating, tightening
like a spider web thread,
and I gently covered my chest with the palm of my hand

It felt like a part of me bleeding,
like every part of me leaving—
even the God I believe in.
I thought in secret,
"Is this what they call grieving?"

I was bobbing and weaving,
'til I started releasing
so hard I was heaving
from my sobbing and weeping

This was the moment I finally let go,
a moment the floodgates could no longer withhold,
the moment I surrendered
and lost all control,
and let the holy water wash over my soul

Holy water, wholly water,
Cleanse and wash me,
Hold me gently,
Hold me softly,

Jesus wept.
These tears have taught me
to weep is human,
to weep is godly.

When I gave permission for the waves to rise
waters gathered like a choir in the aqueduct of my eyes
singing psalms of lament with each changing tide
baptizing my breath with every bathing sigh

Tears of mercy and justice kissed, rolling down my chin to meet
rivers of righteousness slid round my cheek like a mighty stream
these waters have shown me crying is not a sign of being weak
but Love's persistent flow within us during our time of grief

Holy water, wholly water,
Cleanse and wash me,
Hold me gently,
Hold me softly,

Jesus wept.
These tears have taught me
to weep is human,
to weep is godly.

I am not broken,
I am breaking open,
my heart is learning the art of staying open

No need to fight, to hide inside,
try not to let somebody know

I need to cry and remind my eyes
to see where new life might flow

Tears make my eyes swell
Tears make my eyes well

I feel a little lighter now
I see a little light here now

There's something in the water
that heals more than time can tell

These waters won't recede
until they've watered every seed
and we may be in need
to wash, rinse, and repeat

Holy water, wholly water,
Cleanse and wash me,
Hold me gently,
Hold me softly,

Jesus wept.
These tears have taught me
to weep is human,
to weep is godly.

An Invitation:

If you've been feeling bottled up lately, give yourself permission to feel any heavy or uncomfortable emotions. Without resisting or suppressing any feelings or sensations, pay attention to your body—what you feel and where you feel it. After giving yourself enough time to sit with and process your emotions, write any wisdom or insights that might've emerged.

The Need for Rest and Stillness

A poem for slowing down

Do we worry about not being worry free—
working so much we lose touch of what the work means?
The purpose we had at first is blurring,
no longer discerned with certainty.
We can't keep up with the hurried beat—
like a hurricane, a tornado, an earthquake, we're buried
somewhere between
a nightmare and a dream.
And we need to hear or speak a gentle word of peace,
searching for just a second of sincerity.

But there's too much pressure on our chest, we can barely breathe.
Our mind is crowded, too cloudy, we can barely see.
Surrounded by sound too loud and we can barely hear a voice of clarity.
We've reached our limits of commitments,
we're stretched too thin—
our back is broke against the rope and we're at rope's end,
candle burning at both ends until it has no end.

But that's when . . .

We have nothing else to grasp
and yet
we grasp
for breath

And thank God

we
even
have
breath.

An Invitation:

If you don't prioritize space for your own rest, no one else will do it for you. Set aside some time to find rest and stillness, whether it's five minutes, a day, or a weekend. Consider it a gift to your future self.

Grace Like an Ocean

A prayer for grace

Grace is like an ocean
And the Spirit hovers over the face of these waters
Yet we're not meant to play it safe by the harbor
We are all drawn deeper and farther
Called into relationships to travel seas uncharted

Like raindrops
On our cheeks and our chests
Our tears and our sweat
Connecting our bodies, our blood
Streams of consciousness collected in
Pondering ponds, puddles, swamps, and gutters
Wandering waters so often huddled where we're taught they don't belong

However far from the garden—
Life grows wherever the water flows
In the cracked concrete of a city street
Or even in the desert heat
We can still find the budding of a rose

Only our imagination limits where the Holy Spirit moves
Like a flood
Breaking gates and walls
Baptizing beyond the lines of society
And our comfort zones
The raging waves make mountains and shape diamonds cut from stone
Gentle drops soak the soil where the smallest seed becomes the tallest oak

No place too high or too low, too remote or too close
Grace explodes and unfolds
The tides are ever changing, giving rise to new hope

Remember these waters where it all begins
Where we all belong
All gathered, all called, all sent
Grace is the water in which we all swim.

An Invitation:

For the next 24 hours, pay attention to water. Whether it's while brushing your teeth, showering, washing the dishes, watching rain fall, or having a good cry— reflect on baptism and say a prayer for God's grace. As an expression of gratitude, find ways to offer that gift of grace to yourself and others.

Poems for Growth and New Beginnings

Commercial Break

A poem about self-worth

We interrupt your regularly scheduled programming
for a commercial break
or, for all our sakes, a break from commercials
before it's too late for me to escape
the irresistible urge to splurge on the new shoes with the new shoelaces,
new blue jeans and new T that matches my new blazer,
new watch, new shades, and a new bracelet . . .
consumerism is consuming me
with five easy payments!

But don't gain the world and lose your soul,
you got something inside more beautiful
than all the riches you could own,
don't be bought and sold, don't be bought and sold,
don't be bought and sold, don't be bought and sold.

We try to put a price tag on the priceless
and couldn't tell you what the value of life is,
but if they could sell it, everybody would buy it, that's my guess.

Why do I buy products without thinking of the byproduct?
I think I need it, I want it
until the week after I got it
and then I forget about it.

If I'm honest, confessing, I act as if accessories are necessary
when some folks don't have access to necessities.
Unless I've agreed there's a greed that gets the best of me,
there'll always be a need for those who have less than me.

But don't gain the world and lose your soul,
you got something inside more beautiful
than all the riches you could own,
don't be bought and sold, don't be bought and sold,
don't be bought and sold, don't be bought and sold.

A culture of merchandise
hurts our pocketbooks and purses,
but our heart takes the worst hit
when we worship these purchases.

The more we yearn to gain, the more we waste in this evasive chase,
our search for worth is purposeless until we come to terms with this:

God's love for us is perfect and there ain't no earning it.

So don't gain the world and lose your soul,
you got something inside more beautiful
than all the riches you could own,
don't be bought and sold, don't be bought and sold,
don't be bought and sold, don't be bought and sold.

An Invitation:

Take a break from screens for a few
hours or a few days. Start a new project
or work on an old project that's unfinished.
Take a walk outside. Explore, experiment,
express. Go on a new adventure.

Let There Begin

A poem about starting and ending and starting again

Let there be, let there be, let there begin . . .

Always new beginnings,
Even when it seems like the end,
Something will always begin again and again.

We think we've reached the limit, finished, maybe even a death . . .
But we don't know what to call or name whatever might be next.

What is our world
If not a dream called into being?
Inside every seed is everything needed to be a tree,
Waiting achingly to break free.
Every drop of water is part of oceans, rivers, streams.
And before the mightiest mountain peaks
There was only rising dust that our eyes could barely see.

It's in the very air we breathe.

So what dream is right here, stirring in you, stirring in me?
Asking to be born,
Asking for permission,
A vision asking for provision to take shape and take form?
Begging you, beckoning you to not just sorta kinda do it,
But to be a conduit to start a movement.

And to let there be, let there be, let there begin again.

An Invitation:

Write a letter to your future self.
What questions do you have? For extra
credit bonus points, write a letter to your
younger self and offer words of advice
and encouragement. See how the two
letters relate to each other.

Dreamer's Manifesto

A poem about dreams

There's a fire deep inside us.
Our heart is roaring like a lion,
Spirit soaring like an eagle,
With a fist to the sky screaming, "Power to the people!"
We know good will triumph over evil,
That's why we reach high even when we feel low!

Yeah, that's right! This here is our credo:
Mandated to be greater than even our greatest hero!
No one's as special, unique, or as rare as you—
Go on and be the best you can be,
I dare you!

Don't let nothing stop you,
Don't let nothing scare you,
Don't fear to die, don't fear to live,
Don't fear to rise, don't fear to fall,
If there's any fear at all, any fear that's true,
It's the fear that you might really do what you came here to do.

And that's . . .

Dream big! Dream like a little kid!
Dream you can do things that nobody ever did!
You gotta dream, dream, dream!
You gotta dream, dream, dream!

They think I'm sleeping, but I'm scheming like I'm a genius
Seeking life-timeless achievements:
Deep sea diving, mountain climbing, flying higher skyward,
Wingless, unifying dreams to real life
Until it feels like they're seamless yet

It seems as if we've been jaded and deceived
With trading purpose and meaning for comfort and convenience,
But for what it's worth, I'm searching for creative freedom
To make something out of nothing, something we can make believe in!
'Cuz I know it takes a childlike faith
To birth and raise a dream when the haters always try to
Change your angels into demons.

So don't choke down that hopeful passion that you have inside,
Don't try to tame the fire, as its flames have died,
Dream wild and awake with your bright eyes open wide
For life is but a dream only if you dream alive!

We gotta . . .

Dream big! Dream like a little kid!
Dream you can do things that nobody ever did!
You gotta dream, dream, dream!
You gotta dream, dream, dream!

We the dreamers,
In order to form a more perfect universe,
Promise to dream big!
To begin a revolution,
A rapid eye movement
To envision vibrant, vivid images,
Alive and thriving with vigor and vim,
As they live in us we live in them.

Breathing being into things never seen or said before,
Resurrecting that which was desolate and dead before,
Stretching our imagination until it gets sore,
An endeavor better than any human effort ever
Yet even more!

As the Spirit empowers our personality with vitality,
Allowing our unprecedented dreams to be present reality,
Until the truth is unquestionable,
The impossible is inevitable,
The unfathomable is actual,
And our hands can hold the untouchable and intangible,

We will dream those dangerous dreams,
Courageously, boldly, and brazenly,
No matter how crazy it seems, we will dream insanely

Giant dreams
Strong, mighty, and free,
Gravity-defiant dreams
We will dream marvelously, miraculously, extravagantly, intergalactic
dreams.
Not fast asleep, but traveling faster than any dream catcher can capture,
Our surpassing that which ears have heard and eyes have seen:

We will dream everlastingly,
We will dream passionately,
We will dream a masterpiece.
We will dream,
We will dream,
We will dream,
BIG.

An Invitation:

Write, paint, draw, or dance in
response to these questions:

What is your biggest dream?

What do you think will happen next?

How can you share your
dreams with others?

Acknowledgements

I'm grateful for my beautiful parents, James and Juliet, who were the very first to impart the resilient love, faith, and joy that helped shape many of the poems in this book.

I'm grateful for my big sister, Colette, who was my childhood accomplice in creativity—crafts, coloring, and kitchen concoctions—during the endless hours she babysat me.

I'm grateful for my nieces and nephews, Adrian, Estevan, Maya, Kiera, and Arianna, who fill me with hope and inspiration. You remind me of the world that's possible.

I'm grateful for my teachers, mentors, and friends who have laughed and cried with me, who have offered infinite healing and wisdom, who have believed in me even when I didn't believe in myself.

You all help me rise higher and I only hope to do the same for you.